Title: *Micah 6:8: A Prophetic Bridge to Jesus*
Written by: Christian A. Dickinson
Illustrations by: Learning Engineered LLC
Published by: Learning Engineered Publishing

Library of Congress Control Number: 2025936011
ISBN (Print): 978-1-965741-31-3

First Edition: 2025

Printed & Created in: United States of America
Text and Illustration Copyright © 2025

Learning Engineered Publishing is a division of Learning Engineered LLC and a subsidiary of Carpe Diem Unlimited Holdings, Inc.

LEARNING ENGINEERED
PUBLISHING

Contents

Dedication

To honor David Victor Dickinson, my father.

Preface

In a quiet moment coaching a struggling athlete, I saw Micah 6:8 come alive. She faced unfair criticism, yet chose forgiveness over bitterness—reflecting God's call to **"act justly, love mercy, and walk humbly with your God."**

This verse isn't just a moral guide—it's a **prophetic bridge**, pointing from the heart of the Old Testament to the Gospel's fulfillment in Jesus.

I'm not a theologian or scholar. I'm a coach, a mentor, a disciple of Christ—sharing how Micah 6:8 has shaped my journey, and how it can shape yours.

In eighth-century Judah, corruption and empty rituals masked God's desire for *transformed hearts*, not religious transactions. Micah saw beyond the sacrifices to a Savior who would one day embody **justice**, **mercy**, and **humility**.

This book isn't an academic study—it's a **practical guide** to living Micah 6:8 in everyday faith. When Jesus spared a woman caught in sin (John 8:1–11), He fulfilled Micah's call, showing *mercy that restores*. His life weaves a divine thread through Scripture, connecting the cries of the Old Covenant to the grace of the New Covenant.

These pages invite you to walk that bridge. Through stories, reflections, and Scripture, discover how justice, mercy, and humility all point to Jesus—and how they can transform your life.

I pray this journey encourages you to **act justly** in your choices, **love mercy** in your relationships, and **walk humbly** with the God who walks with you.

How to Read This Book

Picture the Samaritan woman at the well, meeting Jesus and finding *living water* (John 4:7–26). This book invites you to encounter **Micah 6:8**—*"act justly, love mercy, walk humbly with your God"*—as a call to live out Christ's transformative grace.

Each chapter unpacks how justice, mercy, and humility—rooted in the Old Testament—come alive in Jesus. Here's how to engage deeply with this journey.

For Individual Study

Open Your Heart Approach Micah 6:8 as a *living invitation*, not just an ancient verse.

Reflect Deeply Answer each chapter's questions to connect justice, mercy, and humility to your daily life.

Seek Jesus Notice how every principle points to Christ's life, death, and resurrection.

Go Slowly Let God's truth sink in—one chapter at a time.

Act on It Transformation is the goal. Ask: *How can I stand for justice today? Where can I show mercy? Am I walking humbly with God?*

For Small Groups & Bible Studies

Prepare Ahead Read the chapter and jot down insights before meeting.

Pray First Ask God to guide your time with His Spirit.

Share Honestly Use the reflection questions to spark open, authentic conversation.

Find Jesus Trace how Micah's call reflects Christ's character in each chapter.

Live It Out Challenge each other to act—perhaps by serving a local need or advocating for someone overlooked.

Close in Prayer Commit to living Micah 6:8, and encouraging one another in faith.

Introduction: A Verse, A Song, A Revelation

When I was a kid, my dad didn't just read Scripture—he sang it. One of his favorites was Micah 6:8.

I can still hear his voice, the steady rhythm of his guitar, the words set to melody:

> **He has shown thee, O man, what is good, and what the Lord requires of thee... to do justly, and to love mercy, and to walk humbly with thy God...**

It was more than a song to him—it was the way he lived. But at the time, I didn't fully grasp its significance.

A Verse at the Funeral

When my dad passed away unexpectedly, I was 17. My mother wanted to place his Bible in the coffin with him, opened to Micah 6:8. She asked me to retrieve it.

I remember standing there, holding his Bible, looking down at the familiar verse. It was underlined in black ink, the lines slightly uneven from a ballpoint pen pressed by a steady, faithful hand:

> *He hath shewed thee, O man, what is good; and what doth the Lord require of thee, but to do justly, and to love mercy, and to walk humbly with thy God?* — **Micah 6:8 (KJV)**

I knew the verse. I knew the melody my dad had set to it. I knew that it had shaped the way he lived his life.

But at 17, I didn't yet understand it.

To me, Micah 6:8 was a moral checklist—a good rule for life, a reminder to be fair, kind, and humble. I carried it with me in memory, in song, in sentiment.

What I didn't realize was that it would take 30 years before I finally saw it for what it truly was.

A Revelation 30 Years in the Making

Decades later, I found myself returning to Micah 6:8, but this time, something shifted.

I had spent a lifetime believing this verse was about personal virtue, but suddenly, I saw something much deeper.

Micah 6:8 wasn't just a call to moral living—it was a *prophetic declaration of the Gospel*.

Micah wasn't merely telling Israel to behave better—he was pointing ahead to Jesus.

For years, I had seen Micah 6:8 as a standalone command. But now, I could see it as part of a much bigger story—one that culminated in Christ.

Micah, writing in a time of corruption and empty religious rituals, wasn't just calling Judah to live ethically. He was revealing God's desire for true transformation—not religious transactions, but hearts changed by justice, mercy, and humility.

And I had missed the most important part:

The *justice* Micah preached wasn't just about fairness—it was fulfilled in Jesus, the One who embodied perfect righteousness and came to bring restoration, not condemnation.

The *mercy* Micah commanded wasn't just kindness—it was foreshadowing the grace Jesus would pour out on sinners, extending forgiveness to those who least deserved it.

The *humility* Micah called for wasn't just modesty—it was the very posture of Jesus, who, though He was God, humbled Himself to walk among us, to serve, and to lay down His life.

Micah 6:8 wasn't merely about Israel's failure—it was about *God's future redemption*. And after 40 years of reading this verse, I finally understood.

The Song Still Plays

Looking back now, I can see it—my dad's faith was never just a song. It was his life, his walk, his testimony.

And though I didn't fully understand it then, I see it now.

Micah 6:8 wasn't just a verse he loved.

It was his way of pointing me to Jesus—even before I realized it.

And now, decades later, I find myself humming that same song.

What This Book Is—And What It's Not

Just to be clear, I'm not a theologian, scholar, or biblical historian. I'm a husband, a father, a coach, a mentor, and a lifelong disciple of Jesus Christ.

This book isn't an academic theological study—it's a reflection on how Micah 6:8 has shaped my journey and how it can shape yours.

I'm not here to present a deep, scholarly exegesis of Micah or Old Testament prophecy. Instead, I want to share a journey of discovery—one that took decades for me to fully understand what my father had been singing about all along.

This book is for those who, like me, want to explore how Micah 6:8 connects to Jesus—not through theological debates, but through real-life faith.

My hope is that this book will encourage you, challenge you, and most of all, help you walk more deeply in *justice*, *mercy*, and *humility*—not just as values, but as a way of following Jesus.

Micah's words weren't just for ancient Judah—they are for us. And now, as we walk through these pages, may you see Micah 6:8 not just as a command, but as a *glimpse of Jesus*.

Chapter 1

Micah's Vision—A Glimpse of Grace

M icah wasn't born into power. He was no priest or royal advisor like Isaiah. A prophet from a small, rural town, he was an ordinary man called to deliver an extraordinary message. In his day, justice was perverted, mercy forgotten, and humility mocked. The wealthy exploited the poor, leaders took bribes, and religious officials preached a hollow faith riddled with ritual and corruption. Yet, amid this darkness, Micah saw something greater: grace.

A Nation on the Brink

In the 8th century B.C., Israel and Judah faced immense upheaval. The Assyrian Empire, a brutal force, was swallowing nations whole. The northern kingdom of Israel was crumbling and would soon fall in 722 B.C. Judah, the southern kingdom, was on a similar path, trusting in wealth, power, and empty religious practices rather than in God. Leaders were corrupt, the poor were oppressed, and complacency reigned.

Micah's message cut through: judgment was coming.

> **"Hear this, you leaders of Jacob, you rulers of Israel, who despise justice and distort all that is right; who build Zion with bloodshed, and Jerusalem with wickedness"** (Micah 3:9–10, NIV).

The elite believed their wealth and rituals secured God's favor, but Micah saw their hearts were far from Him.

More Than Religion—A Call to Transformation

Micah didn't oppose the temple or sacrifices—he opposed empty religion, where rituals replaced *justice, mercy,* and *humility.* His radical call in Micah 6:8 pierced the noise:

> **"He has shown you, O mortal, what is good. And what does the Lord require of you? To act justly and to love mercy and to walk humbly with your God"** (NIV).

God didn't want hollow sacrifices; He wanted transformed hearts. This wasn't new—it echoed God's timeless call—but Judah, like us, needed a wake-up call.

A Bridge to Jesus

Micah 6:8 isn't just a moral command; it points to Jesus. Micah wasn't calling people to try harder but to look forward to Someone greater. *He is justice,* fulfilling the law perfectly. *He is mercy,* extending grace to the undeserving. *He is humility,* humbling Himself to death on a cross. Centuries later, Jesus echoed Micah's vision:

> **"The Spirit of the Lord is on me, because he has anointed me to proclaim good news to the poor... to set the oppressed free"** (Luke 4:18, NIV).

Jesus didn't just preach Micah's message—He lived it perfectly.

Why This Still Matters Today

Micah's words resonate today in a world where justice is distorted, mercy is seen as weakness, and pride is celebrated. Like Judah, we can fall into empty religion, attending church but neglecting to *live out* justice, mercy, and humility. Micah 6:8 invites us to *embody* the Gospel, not just believe it.

Practically:

- *Acting justly* might mean advocating for a coworker unfairly passed over for a promotion due to bias or volunteering at a local shelter to support the marginalized.

- *Loving mercy* could involve forgiving a family member who hurt you, even when it feels unjust, or offering kindness to a stranger who can't repay you.

- *Walking humbly* might mean admitting you were wrong in a disagreement, choosing reconciliation over pride.

These actions reflect Micah's call to live the Gospel in everyday choices, transforming our faith from ritual to reality.

Reflection Questions

1. How can you act justly in your community, as Micah challenged Judah's leaders (Micah 3:9–10)?

2. Is justice about fairness, or does it involve restoring others, as Jesus did with the poor and oppressed (Luke 4:18)?

3. Where do you struggle to show mercy, knowing Judah's failure to love it (Micah 6:8)?

4. Do you demand justice for others but expect mercy for yourself?

5. What does walking humbly look like in your daily life, inspired by Jesus' example (Luke 4:18)?

6. Are there areas where pride, like Judah's trust in wealth, prevents you from surrendering to God?

Final Thought: A Glimpse of Grace

The question isn't whether we believe in Micah 6:8, but whether we're living it. Micah stood at a crossroads, seeing a nation lost but glimpsing a future where justice, mercy, and humility would be fulfilled in Jesus. His message wasn't just for Judah—it's for us. We live in that redemption.

Chapter 2

Loving Mercy—Jesus, the Embodiment of Grace

M icah's world was harsh. Mercy was scarce, the powerful crushed the weak, debts were ruthlessly collected, and forgiveness was a transaction reserved for those who could pay. Religious leaders turned mercy into a system of sacrifices, a way to appease God while living selfishly.

But Micah saw through it, proclaiming a radical truth: God didn't just want people to *show* mercy—He wanted them to *love* it.

To love mercy is to delight in grace, to extend it without keeping score, and to see it as God's heartbeat. In this, Micah unknowingly pointed to Jesus, the embodiment of mercy.

Mercy in Micah's Time

In ancient Israel, justice often meant punishment—steal, and you paid back with interest; sin, and you faced retribution. Undeserved kindness was rare. Micah's audience was religious but reduced faith to rules and rituals, missing God's heart.

When Micah said, **"Love mercy"** (Micah 6:8), he called them to reorient their understanding. Mercy wasn't weakness or a transaction—it was God's character.

Mercy doesn't stand alone; it intertwines with *justice* and *humility*.

- *Justice* demands fairness.

- *Mercy* tempers it with compassion, choosing forgiveness over retribution.

- *Humility* enables mercy by reminding us we're all recipients of grace.

Together, these three reflect God's heart: *Justice restores what's broken, mercy heals the undeserving, and humility aligns us with God's will.*

Jesus: The Mercy of God in Flesh

Jesus didn't just preach mercy—He lived it. He touched lepers (Matthew 8:1–3), dined with sinners (Luke 19:1–10), and forgave the unforgivable (John 8:1–11).

His parables, like the *Prodigal Son* and the *Good Samaritan*, redefined who deserved grace.

On the cross, Jesus embodied ultimate mercy, taking the punishment we deserved so we could receive grace we could never earn.

Micah's call to love mercy found its fulfillment in Him.

Why Do We Struggle to Love Mercy?

Loving mercy is hard. Forgiving those who hurt us feels unjust. *Justice satisfies our sense of fairness; mercy costs us our pride.*

But Micah 6:8 doesn't say *"show mercy"*—it says *"love mercy."* That's a deeper call. To choose grace over revenge. Forgiveness over bitterness. Compassion over judgment.

We can love mercy because God first loved us:

"Because of his great love for us, God, who is rich in mercy, made us alive with Christ even when we were dead in transgressions" (Ephesians 2:4–5, NIV).

How to Love Mercy Like Jesus

Receive God's Mercy Fully Reflect on a moment God forgave you—perhaps a failure or broken promise—and how His grace restored you. Have you embraced that you don't earn His love?

Extend Mercy Freely Jesus ate with sinners and healed outcasts. Show mercy by listening without judgment or helping someone despite their past. *Mercy isn't earned—it's given.*

See Mercy as Strength The world calls mercy weak, but Jesus calls it power. Forgiveness takes courage. Serving the hurting requires compassion. *It's Christ's power in us that makes mercy possible.*

Reflection Questions

1. How has God's mercy, as seen in Jesus' life (Luke 19:1–10), transformed your perspective?

2. Do you fully grasp the depth of grace you've received (Ephesians 2:4–5)?

3. Who in your life needs your mercy right now, as Micah called Judah to love it (Micah 6:8)?

4. Is there someone you need to forgive? What's holding you back?

5. Do you delight in mercy—or do you struggle to extend it?

6. How can you cultivate a heart that loves

mercy like Jesus does?

Final Thought: Loving Mercy Is Loving Jesus

To love mercy is to love Christ.

Micah's call wasn't just a command—it was a prophecy fulfilled.

When we live in mercy, we don't just follow a rule—we follow Jesus Himself.

Chapter 3

Walking Humbly—Jesus, the Perfect Example

Micah's words were simple yet profound:

> **"...walk humbly with your God"**
> (Micah 6:8).

Humility isn't thinking *less* of yourself—it's thinking of yourself *less*. It's living fully dependent on God, not success, status, or strength.

The world rewards self-promotion. Judah trusted in wealth and ritual, not in God. Micah called them—and us—to a better way.

Humility in Micah's Time

Judah's pride was their downfall.

- Religious leaders believed rituals earned God's favor.

- Wealthy elites exploited the poor (Micah 2:1–2).

- Rulers formed alliances with Assyria—alliances that backfired.

Micah warned:

> **"Shall I come before the Lord with burnt offerings?... Will the Lord be pleased with thousands of rams?"**
> (Micah 6:6–7, NIV).

God didn't want more sacrifice. He wanted *surrendered hearts.*

Jesus: The Model of True Humility

Jesus lived in humility from beginning to end.

- Born in a manger (Luke 2:7).

- Announced to shepherds, not kings.

- Washed His disciples' feet (John 13:3–5).

- Died with surrender on His lips: **"Not my will, but yours be done"** (Luke 22:42, NIV).

Jesus redefined greatness:

> **"Whoever wants to become great among you must be your servant"** (Matthew 20:26, NIV).

Why Do We Struggle with Humility?

We often trust our strength over God's. Pride blinds us to our need. But Micah's call to walk humbly isn't a moment—it's a *way of life*.

Jesus stooped to serve. He laid down His rights. He invites us to live the same way (Philippians 2:5–8).

How to Walk Humbly Like Jesus

Recognize Your Need for God Pride says, "I've got this." Humility says, "God, I need You." Pray instead of pushing through alone (James 4:6).

Submit to God's Will Trust God's plan, even when it disrupts yours (Luke 22:42).

Serve Others Before Yourself Mentor a younger colleague. Help a neighbor with chores. Follow Jesus in humble service (John 13:14–15).

Stay Teachable When someone corrects you, thank them. A humble heart welcomes growth.

Reflection Questions

1. Where do you struggle with humility, as Judah did (Micah 6:6–7)?

2. Are you trusting your own strength over God's provision?

3. How does Jesus' humility challenge your

view of success (John 13:3–5)?

4. What step can you take this week to walk humbly, like Jesus (Luke 22:42)?

5. Is there an area where God is calling you to surrender?

Final Thought: Walking in Jesus' Footsteps

Humility isn't weakness—it's the heart of discipleship. Micah called Judah to walk humbly. Jesus walked that path for us. Now, we follow in His footsteps.

Chapter 4

The Heart of God's Call

Micah 6:8 is more than a powerful Old Testament verse—it's a bridge between the Old and New Covenants, a call to live *God's heart*. At first glance, it seems simple:

"Act justly, love mercy, walk humbly with your God."

But beneath these words lies a profound truth, pointing beyond rules to the One who *fulfills* them.

Micah spoke to people lost in ritual, revealing God's desire for hearts aligned with His. This chapter explores how Micah 6:8 unveils *God's character*, how Israel missed it, and how Jesus embodies it, inviting us to live His justice, mercy, and humility *today*.

A People Obsessed with Rituals

In Micah's time, eighth-century Judah thrived with religious activity. The temple in Jerusalem bustled with priests offering sacrifices—*lambs, rams, and doves*—while festivals like Passover drew crowds waving palm branches. Yet corruption festered:

- merchants **cheated** with false scales (Micah 6:11),

- judges **took bribes** (Micah 3:11),

- and the poor were **trampled** (Micah 2:2).

The people believed their offerings secured God's favor, treating faith like a transaction.

Micah shattered this illusion:

"Will the Lord be pleased with thousands of rams, with ten thousand rivers of olive oil?" (Micah 6:7)

God didn't want *grand sacrifices*; He wanted **hearts reflecting His justice, mercy, and humility**.

This wasn't new—God had always sought **devotion over ritual**, as seen in His call to love and obey:

"And now, Israel, what does the Lord your God ask of you but to fear the Lord your God, to walk in obedience to him, to love him, to serve the Lord your God with all your heart and with all your soul?"(Deuteronomy 10:12–13)

Ritual Over Relationship Today

The temptation to prioritize *ritual over relationship* persists in modern Christianity. We may attend church weekly, sing worship songs, or post Bible verses online, yet harbor resentment or neglect the hurting.

A megachurch might boast packed services and polished programs, but ignore the homeless outside its doors. A Christian might pray daily yet dismiss a coworker's pain—assuming spiritual disciplines alone please God.

Like Judah, we risk reducing faith to checklists—*tithing, volunteering, fasting*—while missing **God's heart**. Micah's wake-up call echoes: God desires **justice in our actions**, **mercy in our hearts**, and **humility before Him**, not just religious performance.

"Learn to do right; seek justice. Defend the oppressed. Take up the cause of the fatherless; plead the case of the widow." (Isaiah 1:17)

Faith without love is hollow.

Jesus: The Fulfillment of Micah's Call

Micah 6:8 is a bridge, and **Jesus is its destination**. He didn't merely teach justice, mercy, and humility—**He lived them**.

- **Jesus acted justly**, defending the outcast Samaritan woman at the well (John 4:7–26) and confronting the hypocrisy of religious leaders (Matthew 23:23–24). His justice came not through power but through *sacrifice*, proclaiming *freedom for the oppressed* (Luke 4:18).

- **Jesus loved mercy**, eating with tax collectors (Mark 2:15–17), forgiving a woman caught in sin (John 8:1–11), and praying for His crucifiers (Luke 23:34).

- **Jesus walked humbly**, leaving heaven's glory to *serve* (John 13:3–5), surrendering to the Father's will (Luke 22:42), and *dying for us* (Philippians 2:6–8).

Jesus didn't *replace* Micah's call—**He fulfilled it**, *embodying God's heart perfectly*.

Living Micah 6:8 Today

We no longer live under the Old Covenant's sacrifices or rituals. **Jesus is our sacrifice**, our righteousness, our way to God. Yet **Micah 6:8 remains a guide**—not to earn salvation, but to *reflect the One who saved us*.

- We **act justly** by advocating for the marginalized—perhaps volunteering at a shelter or speaking against workplace unfairness.

- We **love mercy** by forgiving a friend who hurt us or listening to a stranger's story.

- We **walk humbly** by admitting our flaws, seeking God's will over our own—like a parent praying for patience instead of control.

In a Cape Town township, I once saw a pastor feed orphans with his own hands. His clothes were worn and his hands calloused, but his heart radiated compassion. *That, too, was Micah 6:8 in action.*

Micah looked forward to Christ; we look back, *empowered by His Spirit* to live His way.

Invitation to Live God's Heart

Pause to reflect on **Micah 6:8**

How is God calling you to *act justly, love mercy, walk humbly*?

- Gather with friends in a quiet place to share a time you chose mercy over judgment—like forgiving a betrayal.

- Journal a moment when humility drew you closer to God, perhaps admitting a mistake.

- Sketch a bridge to recall Jesus as the *destination*.

- Create a keepsake—a card with **Micah 6:8** written on it.

- Read **Luke 4:18–19**: Where is Jesus calling you to bring justice or mercy?

- Pray: *Lord, shape my heart to reflect Yours.*

- Serve someone in need—a neighbor, a coworker—reflecting **Christ's love**.

These steps align you with *His rhythm*.

Closing Reflection

Micah 6:8 is God's heartbeat—a call beyond rituals to a life of **justice**, **mercy**, and **humility**. Judah's sacrifices, our modern checklists—*all fall short without love*. Jesus fulfilled Micah's words, inviting us to follow.

That Cape Town pastor, the Samaritan woman's encounter, and moments of surrender all point to Christ's way.

Chapter 5

Justice—The Heart of God

Justice is more than a human ideal—it's a reflection of *God's character*. Micah's call to **"act justly"** (Micah 6:8) wasn't about mere fairness; it was about *restoring what was broken, defending the vulnerable*, and *revealing God's righteousness*.

In eighth-century Judah, justice had become a tool for power, crushing the poor while the powerful prospered. Micah confronted this spiritual disease, pointing to a Savior who would embody justice. Jesus didn't just teach justice—**He is justice**, fulfilling Micah's call through His life, death, and resurrection.

This chapter explores justice as God's heartbeat: *perverted in Micah's time, embodied by Jesus, and lived out by us today*.

Justice in Micah's Time

The Hebrew word *mishpat* means *making things right*—restoring order, defending the weak, and aligning life with God's righteousness. But Judah had corrupted *mishpat*.

- Wealthy landowners **seized family fields** through deceit, leaving widows homeless (Micah 2:1–2).

- Judges **accepted bribes** to favor the rich, twisting verdicts against the poor (Micah 3:11).

- False prophets **preached prosperity for profit**, silencing cries for truth (Micah 3:5).

- The temple overflowed with sacrifices, yet the marketplace thrived on **dishonest scales** (Micah 6:11).

Micah's warning was stark:

"Should you not embrace justice, you who hate good and love evil?" (Micah 3:1)

God's anger burned not just at their actions but at *hearts far from His*—offering rituals instead of righteousness.

True justice, Micah declared, *reflects God's heart, not human greed*.

Justice in Our Time

Judah's failure echoes in modern Christianity, where we risk prioritizing *comfort over justice*.

We may attend church, give offerings, or post Bible verses online, yet ignore the homeless person outside our sanctuary. A Christian business owner might pray faithfully but pay workers unfairly, mirroring Judah's dishonest scales. Congregations might host vibrant worship services while neglecting systemic injustices—poverty, discrimination—that harm their communities.

Like Judah, we can fall into the trap of *religious performance*, checking spiritual boxes while ignoring the vulnerable. Micah's call remains: **God desires justice that restores, not rituals that soothe our conscience**.

> **"Learn to do right; seek justice. Defend the oppressed."** (Isaiah 1:16–17)

Faith without action is empty—a lesson as urgent now as in Micah's day.

Jesus: The Just One

Micah's vision of justice pointed to **Jesus**, its perfect fulfillment. Jesus brought justice through **mercy**, not force.

In John 8:1–11, when Pharisees demanded a woman caught in adultery be stoned, Jesus offered *divine justice*:

"Let any one of you who is without sin be first to throw a stone."

His mercy restored her, giving her a new path.

Jesus confronted injustice boldly, overturning tables in the temple (Matthew 21:12–13), where religious leaders exploited worshipers for profit—turning God's house into a *"den of robbers"*. That phrase referred to a place where bandits hid after committing crimes. In other words, Jesus exposed the temple system as a cover for injustice.

He declared, **"My house will be a house of prayer"**, restoring its purpose.

Most profoundly, Jesus fulfilled justice on the cross. **"He was pierced for our transgressions... the punishment that brought us peace was on him."** (Isaiah 53:5)

By taking our sin, **He made things right**—*embodying mishpat through sacrifice*.

6-Week Small Group & Bible Study Guide

How to Use This Guide

This **6-week study guide** is designed to help small groups, Bible studies, and individuals go deeper into **Micah 6:8 and its fulfillment in Jesus Christ**. Each session includes:

- A Chapter to Read Before the Meeting

- Discussion Questions to Spark Conversation

- Reflection Prompts for Personal Growth

- A Closing Prayer & Practical "Next Steps"

MICAH 6:8

6-Week Study Plan

Week 1: Micah's Vision—A Glimpse of Grace

Read: Chapter 1
Key Focus: How does Micah 6:8 connect to God's greater plan for salvation?
Discussion Questions:

1. What stood out to you about Micah's time and message?

2. How does Micah's call differ from mere religious ritual?

3. Why do you think God values justice, mercy, and humility over sacrifices?

Prayer Focus: Ask God to reveal how He is shaping your heart toward these three values.
Next Steps: Spend the next week reflecting on **a moment in your life when you saw justice, mercy, or humility at work.**

Week 2: The Call to Justice—Jesus, the Just One

Read: Chapter 2 **Key Focus:** What does **true justice** look like according to Jesus? **Discussion Questions:**

1. How does biblical justice differ from worldly justice?

2. How did Jesus model justice in His ministry?

3. Where is God calling you to pursue justice in your own life?

Prayer Focus: Ask God to help you **see injustice through His eyes** and respond in love. **Next Steps:** Identify **one area in your life** where you can **stand for justice** (at work, in relationships, or your community).

MICAH 6:8

Week 3: Loving Mercy—Jesus, the Embodiment of Grace

Read: Chapter 3 **Key Focus:** How do we love mercy as Jesus did? **Discussion Questions:**

1. How did Jesus demonstrate radical mercy?

2. Why is it often hard to extend mercy to others?

3. Where in your life is God calling you to show **undeserved mercy**?

Prayer Focus: Pray for a **merciful heart** that mirrors Christ's love. **Next Steps:** This week, **forgive someone, show kindness, or extend grace** where you normally wouldn't.

MICAH 6:8

Week 4: Walking Humbly—Jesus, the Perfect Example

Read: Chapter 4
Key Focus: What does it truly mean to walk humbly with God?
Discussion Questions:

1. How did Jesus model humility in His life and ministry?

2. What is the biggest **barrier** to humility in today's culture?

3. How can we cultivate a **lifestyle** of humility?

Prayer Focus: Ask God to help you **surrender pride and depend fully on Him**.
Next Steps: Intentionally **serve someone this week** without expecting recognition.

MICAH 6:8

Week 5: Micah 6:8—The Bridge Between Covenants

Read: Chapter 5 **Key Focus:** How does Micah 6:8 **connect the Old Testament to Jesus**? **Discussion Questions:**

1. How does Jesus fulfill Micah's vision of justice, mercy, and humility?

2. Why is it important to read the Old Testament through a Christ-centered lens?

3. What does it mean to live in the **fulfillment of Micah 6:8** today?

Prayer Focus: Thank God for **revealing Christ through Micah's prophecy**. **Next Steps:** Identify a way to actively live out Micah 6:8 in your community this week.

MICAH 6:8

Week 6: Living Micah 6:8 in a Modern World

Key Focus: How do we live out Micah 6:8 in our daily lives? **Discussion Questions:**

1. What is your biggest takeaway from this study?

2. How has your understanding of Micah 6:8 changed?

3. What **practical commitment** will you make to live out justice, mercy, and humility?

Prayer Focus: Ask God to **help you embody Micah 6:8 in your daily life**. **Next Steps:** Write a **personal commitment statement** about how you will live out Micah 6:8 going forward.

MICAH 6:8

About the Author

Christian A. Dickinson is an author, speaker, and the President & CEO of Learning Engineered Publishing, where he develops faith-based and educational books—including devotionals, Bible commentaries, and children's literature.

With over 20 years of experience as a principal, teacher, and coach, Christian has dedicated his life to mentoring and shaping future generations—a passion that fuels his writing and biblical studies.

His works include *FULL CIRCLE 360: A Devotional for Athletes* and *Jesus Was Funnier Than*

You Think, and he co-authors character-building children's books with his wife, Morgan.

Beyond faith-based writing, his publishing company produces STEM magazines, economic literacy books for classrooms, and non-faith-based parenting resources.

When he's not writing or mentoring, you'll find him spending time with his wife, exploring and playing with their young daughter, or inspiring others through storytelling and leadership.

More by Christian A. Dickinson

I f you enjoyed Micah 6:8, you may also appreciate these Christ-centered resources:

Jesus Was Funnier Than You Think: Unlocking His Wit, Wisdom, and Unexpected Humor
A fresh look at the wit and humor of Jesus Christ — revealing the brilliant, joyful ways He taught truth and disarmed pride.

Every Tear Remembered: God's Presence in Our Grief
A reflection on sorrow, healing, and hope through the lens of God's enduring love.

The Curse of Time: Time Began When Eternity Broke

A theological and personal exploration of time as a consequence of sin—not a neutral part of creation. Drawing from Scripture, Church Fathers, and moments of divine encounter, this book challenges the assumption that time was God's original design and invites readers to rediscover the eternal now of God's presence.

Roar of 'Ēzer: Reclaiming God's Vision for Women's Strength

From Eden's garden to the early church, God named women 'ēzer—rescuer, strength-bearer, equal partner in His image. This compelling biblical exploration invites women to rise, not as shadows but as co-laborers in God's kingdom. With Scripture, story, and a call to courage, Roar of 'Ēzer reveals that women were never meant to shrink. They were always meant to roar.

The Prophetic Equation: Thirty Prophets. One Christ. Zero Coincidence.
An exploration of how thirty prophetic voices across centuries, kingdoms, and crises converge with stunning precision in Jesus Christ — revealing that Scripture is not random, but a masterpiece of divine design.

It's All or Nothing: How Jesus Raised the Standard from Tithing to Full Surrender
A biblical commentary challenging traditional views of tithing by exploring Jesus' call to radical, Spirit-led generosity.

FULL CIRCLE: PREGAME — A Devotional Series for Athletes
Before the whistle blows and the lights come up, PREGAME challenges

athletes to prepare their hearts as well as their bodies. With powerful stories, Scripture reflections, and real talk from the locker room, Coach Dickinson and Anthony "Diso" Paradiso equip competitors to lead with faith, play with integrity, and honor Christ in every moment.

www.ingramcontent.com/pod-product-compliance
Lightning Source LLC
Chambersburg PA
CBHW031255120626
46545CB00007B/2833